TROWBRIDGE LEA

This book

Francis Frith's
GLAMORGAN

Photographic Memories

Francis Frith's
GLAMORGAN

Revised Edition of an Original Publication by
Aeres Twigg

First published in the United Kingdom in 2002 by
Frith Book Company Ltd

Hardback Edition
ISBN 1-85937-488-3

Revised Paperback Edition 2003
ISBN 1-85937-679-7

Reprinted in Paperback 2005

British Library Cataloguing in Publication Data

Francis Frith's Glamorgan
Aeres Twigg

Frith Book Company Ltd
Frith's Barn, Teffont,
Salisbury, Wiltshire SP3 5QP
Tel: +44 (0) 1722 716 376
Email: info@francisfrith.co.uk
www.francisfrith.co.uk

Cover Image: **Swansea, High Street 1893** 32720t

The colour-tinting is for illustrative purposes only, and is not intended to be historically accurate

Printed and bound in Great Britain

Contents

Francis Frith: *Victorian Pioneer*

FRANCIS FRITH, Victorian founder of the world-famous photographic archive, was a complex and multi-talented man. A devout Quaker and a highly successful Victorian businessman, he was both philosophical by nature and pioneering in outlook.

By 1855 Francis Frith had already established a wholesale grocery business in Liverpool, and sold it for the astonishing sum of £200,000, which is the equivalent today of over £15,000,000. Now a very rich man, he was able to indulge his passion for travel. As a child he had pored over travel books written by early explorers, and his fancy and imagination had been stirred by family holidays to the sublime mountain regions of Wales and Scotland. 'What lands of spirit-stirring and enriching scenes and places!' he had written. He was to return to these scenes of grandeur in later years to 'recapture the thousands of vivid and tender memories', but with a different purpose. Now in his thirties, and captivated by the new science of photography, Frith set out on a series of pioneering journeys to the Nile regions that occupied him from 1856 until 1860.

Intrigue and Adventure

He took with him on his travels a specially-designed wicker carriage that acted as both dark-room and sleeping chamber. These far-flung journeys were packed with intrigue and adventure. In his life story, written when he was sixty-three, Frith tells of being held captive by bandits, and of fighting 'an awful midnight battle to the very point of surrender with a deadly pack of hungry, wild dogs'. Sporting flowing Arab costume, Frith arrived at Akaba by camel sixty years before Lawrence, where he encountered 'desert princes and rival sheikhs, blazing with jewel-hilted swords'.

During these extraordinary adventures he was assiduously exploring the desert regions bordering the Nile and patiently recording the antiquities and peoples with his camera. He was the first photographer to venture beyond the sixth cataract. Africa was still the mysterious 'Dark Continent', and Stanley and Livingstone's historic meeting was a decade into the future. The conditions for picture taking confound belief. He laboured for hours in his wicker dark-room in the sweltering heat of the desert, while the volatile chemicals fizzed dangerously in their trays. Often he was forced to work in remote tombs and caves where conditions were cooler. Back in London he exhibited his photographs and was 'rapturously cheered' by members of the Royal Society. His reputation as a photographer was made overnight. An eminent modern historian has likened their impact on the population of the time to that on our own generation of the first photographs taken on the surface of the moon.

Venture of a Life-Time

Characteristically, Frith quickly spotted the opportunity to create a new business as a specialist publisher of photographs. He lived in an era of immense and sometimes violent change. For the poor in the early part of Victoria's reign work was a drudge and the hours long, and people had precious little free time to enjoy themselves. Most had no transport other than a cart or gig at their disposal, and had not travelled far beyond the boundaries of their own town or village. However,

by the 1870s, the railways had threaded their way across the country, and Bank Holidays and half-day Saturdays had been made obligatory by Act of Parliament. All of a sudden the ordinary working man and his family were able to enjoy days out and see a little more of the world.

With characteristic business acumen, Francis Frith foresaw that these new tourists would enjoy having souvenirs to commemorate their days out. In 1860 he married Mary Ann Rosling and set out with the intention of photographing every city, town and village in Britain. For the next thirty years he travelled the country by train and by pony and trap, producing fine photographs of seaside resorts and beauty spots that were keenly bought by millions of Victorians. These prints were painstakingly pasted into family albums and pored over during the dark nights of winter, rekindling precious memories of summer excursions.

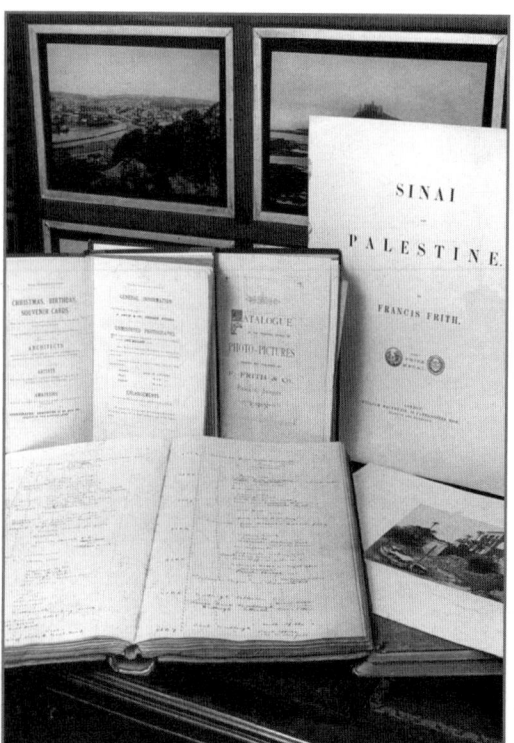

The Rise of Frith & Co

Frith's studio was soon supplying retail shops all over the country. To meet the demand he gathered about him a small team of photographers, and published the work of independent artist-photographers of the calibre of Roger Fenton and Francis Bedford. In order to gain some understanding of the scale of Frith's business one only has to look at the catalogue issued by Frith & Co in 1886: it runs to some 670 pages, listing not only many thousands of views of the British Isles but also many photographs of most European countries, and China, Japan, the USA and Canada – note the sample page shown on page 9 from the hand-written *Frith & Co* ledgers detailing pictures taken. By 1890 Frith had created the greatest specialist photographic publishing company in the world, with over 2,000

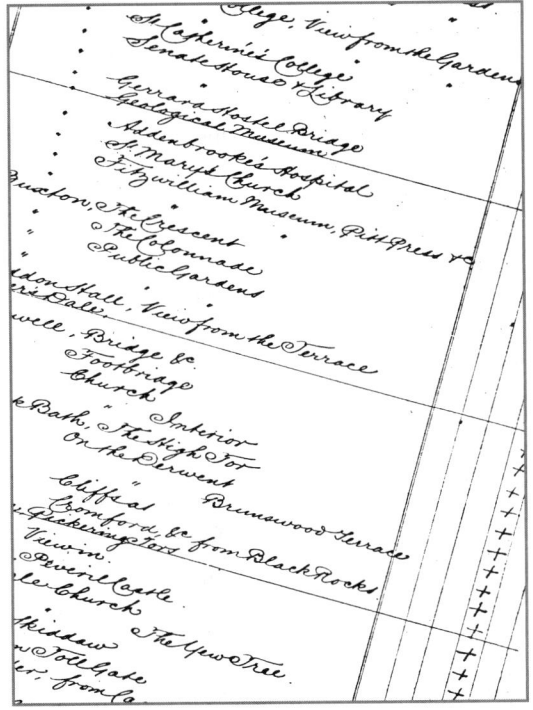

Frith's death, a new card measuring 5.5 x 3.5 inches became the standard format, but it was not until 1902 that the divided back came into being, with address and message on one face and a full-size illustration on the other. *Frith & Co* were in the vanguard of postcard development, and Frith's sons Eustace and Cyril continued their father's monumental task, expanding the number of views offered to the public and recording more and more places in Britain, as the coasts and countryside were opened up to mass travel.

Francis Frith died in 1898 at his villa in Cannes, his great project still growing. The archive he created continued in business for another seventy years. By 1970 it contained over a third of a million pictures of 7,000 cities, towns and villages. The massive photographic record Frith has left to us stands as a living monument to a special and very remarkable man.

outlets – more than the combined number that Boots and W H Smith have today! The picture on the right shows the *Frith & Co* display board at Ingleton in the Yorkshire Dales (left of window). Beautifully constructed with a mahogany frame and gilt inserts, it could display up to a dozen local scenes.

Postcard Bonanza

The ever-popular holiday postcard we know today took many years to develop. In 1870 the Post Office issued the first plain cards, with a pre-printed stamp on one face. In 1894 they allowed other publishers' cards to be sent through the mail with an attached adhesive halfpenny stamp. Demand grew rapidly, and in 1895 a new size of postcard was permitted called the court card, but there was little room for illustration. In 1899, a year after

Frith's Archive: *A Unique Legacy*

FRANCIS FRITH'S legacy to us today is of immense significance and value, for the magnificent archive of evocative photographs he created provides a unique record of change in 7,000 cities, towns and villages throughout Britain over a century and more. Frith and his fellow studio photographers revisited locations many times down the years to update their views, compiling for us an enthralling and colourful pageant of British life and character.

We tend to think of Frith's sepia views of Britain as nostalgic, for most of us use them to conjure up memories of places in our own lives with which we have family associations. It often makes us forget that to Francis Frith they were records of daily life as it was actually being lived in the cities, towns and villages of his day. The Victorian age was one of great and often bewildering change for ordinary people, and though the pictures evoke an impression of slower times, life was as busy and hectic as it is today.

We are fortunate that Frith was a photographer of the people, dedicated to recording the minutiae of everyday life. For it is this sheer wealth of visual data, the painstaking chronicle of changes in dress, transport, street layouts, buildings, housing, engineering and landscape that captivates us so much today. His remarkable images offer us a powerful link with the past and with the lives of our ancestors.

Today's Technology

Computers have now made it possible for Frith's many thousands of images to be accessed almost instantly. In the Frith archive today, each photograph is carefully 'digitised' then stored on a CD Rom. Frith archivists can locate a single photograph amongst thousands within seconds. Views can be catalogued and sorted under a variety of categories of place and content to the immediate benefit of researchers.

Inexpensive reference prints can be created for them at the touch of a mouse button, and a wide range of books and other printed materials assembled and published for a wider, more general readership. The day-to-day workings of the archive are very different from how they were in Francis Frith's time: imagine the herculean task of sorting through eleven tons of glass negatives as Frith had to do to locate a particular sequence of pictures! Yet the archive still prides itself on maintaining the same high standards of excellence laid down by

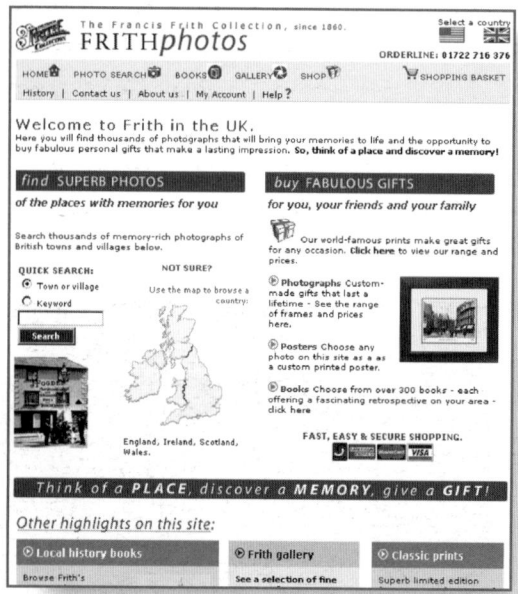

See Frith at www.francisfrith.co.uk

Francis Frith, including the painstaking cataloguing and indexing of every view.

It is curious to reflect on how the internet now allows researchers in America and elsewhere greater instant access to the archive than Frith himself ever enjoyed. Many thousands of individual views can be called up on screen within seconds on one of the Frith internet sites, enabling people living continents away to revisit the streets of their ancestral home town, or view places in Britain where they have enjoyed holidays. Many overseas researchers welcome the chance to view special theme selections, such as transport, sports, costume and ancient monuments.

We are certain that Francis Frith would have heartily approved of these modern developments in imaging techniques, for he himself was always working at the very limits of Victorian photographic technology.

The Value of the Archive Today

Because of the benefits brought by the computer, Frith's images are increasingly studied by social historians, by researchers into genealogy and ancestory, by architects, town planners, and by teachers and schoolchildren involved in local history projects.

In addition, the archive offers every one of us an opportunity to examine the places where we and our families have lived and worked down the years. Highly successful in Frith's own era, the archive is now, a century and more on, entering a new phase of popularity.

The Past in Tune with the Future

Historians consider the Francis Frith Collection to be of prime national importance. It is the only archive of its kind remaining in private ownership and has been valued at a million pounds. However, this figure is now rapidly increasing as digital technology enables more and more people around the world to enjoy its benefits.

Francis Frith's archive is now housed in an historic timber barn in the beautiful village of Teffont in Wiltshire. Its founder would not recognize the archive office as it is today. In place of the many thousands of dusty boxes containing glass plate negatives and an all-pervading odour of photographic chemicals, there are now ranks of computer screens. He would be amazed to watch his images travelling round the world at unimaginable speeds through network and internet lines.

The archive's future is both bright and exciting. Francis Frith, with his unshakeable belief in making photographs available to the greatest number of people, would undoubtedly approve of what is being done today with his lifetime's work. His photographs, depicting our shared past, are now bringing pleasure and enlightenment to millions around the world a century and more after his death.

GLAMORGAN - *An Introduction*

IN EARLY WELSH HISTORY, Glamorgan was a kingdom in its own right. Its name is derived from Morgannwg or Gwlad Morgan, meaning 'Morgan's Land'; Morgannwg was the name of the Marcher Lordship situated between the rivers Nedd and Taf. The Act of Union of 1536 added Gower to Morgannwg to create the new county of Glamorgan. Bordered by Breconshire to the north, Gwent to the east, the sea to the south and Carmarthenshire to the west, it has a large and diverse population.The railway line linking Milford Haven and London runs through the county, and so does the M4 motorway and the A48, the old portway, which roughly follows the route of the Roman road.Today's visitors can marvel at how

the scars of Glamorgan's industrial past are being obliterated - the valleys are becoming green again. But for the more curious there are clues to a much older history. Prehistoric animals, Neolithic tribes, the Celts, the Romans, the Normans and the Vikings have all left their mark on the county. Three hundred years ago the county was mainly agricultural: there were sheep on the hills and woollen mills along the river banks, and there was arable farming in the lowlands - the Gower peninsula and the Vale of Glamorgan. There were small-scale industries: coal was mined and copper was smelted. Sir Humphrey Mackworth had copper smelting works near Neath and brought lead from Cardiganshire to be smelted

there; by 1708 Neath had 12 lead furnaces and 2 copper furnaces. Dr John Lane established copper works at Landore in 1717. Being a better port, Swansea ousted Neath in importance, and by 1750 about half the copper produced in Britain was smelted in the Swansea area.

By 1720 there were 16 iron furnaces using timber from local sources. The Seven Years' War meant an increase in demand and the cessation of supplies from abroad, so blast furnaces were established at Hirwaun and Dowlais. By 1788, blast furnaces were producing 10,000 tons of pig iron annually. Peter Onions, a foreman at Cyfarthfa, discovered the puddling process: this reduced pig iron to malleable or wrought iron, and it became known as 'the Welsh method'.

Coal has been used here since the 13th century, mainly in homes and in the limestone industry. It was mined from shallow pits in Gower and at Neath and Aberavon. In 1695 Sir Henry Mackworth invested in recovering coal; he employed men, women and children. Pit ponies were stabled underground - they were allowed 2 weeks' holiday in the open air during August each year. Merthyr Tydfil became the 'iron capital' of Britain owing to its proximity to the coal mines at the heads of the valleys. As access to Merthyr was difficult even by improved turnpike roads, an act was secured in 1790 for a canal from Merthyr to Cardiff; between 1794 and 1799 four canals were opened, the Glamorganshire, the Neath, the Monmouthshire and the Swansea.

Then came the period of the railway. Brunel built the South Wales railway linking Chepstow and Swansea in 1850, and the Severn tunnel was opened in 1886. What is more important, the railway linked the valleys with the ports. Most of the traffic was from north to south, and coal was the main cargo.

Because of the high tidal range of the Bristol channel, docks were constructed at Cardiff, Penarth and Swansea; in 1889 David Davies and John Cory built Barry Docks, thus depriving Cardiff of the title of largest coal exporting port in the world - in 1913, Barry exported 11.05 million tons of coal to Cardiff's 10.6 million tons.

The industrial revolution brought an influx of people into the county, many from other Welsh counties, and some from different parts of England. Welsh was spoken by the older people, and was kept alive in the chapels and Sunday schools. Then, when Welsh schools were introduced in the 20th century, more young people started speaking Welsh too.

The Museum of Welsh Life, which covers 100

acres at St Fagans, is one of Europe's biggest and most exciting open-air museums. Its collection of buildings recreates 500 years of history. It holds festivals, and employs craftsmen to demonstrate traditional skills. Three new buildings added during this millennium are the decorated medieval church of St Teilo, Tal-y-bont from Pontarddulais, a 1940s prefab, and the House of the Future.

One of Glamorgan's famous sons, Iolo Morgannwg (1747-1826), was born in Lancarfan and died at Flemingstone. A stonemason by trade, he wrote poems in both English and Welsh and helped to found the Unitarian Society in South Wales. It was he who introduced the 'Gorsedd of Bards' to the Eisteddfod. The landed gentry in the county were patrons of Welsh literature. The Triban, a verse form with a distinctive rhyming scheme, is claimed to have been invented by Glamorgan bards. Glamorgan Welsh is distinctive, with the hardening of some consonants and the inclusion of words not common in other counties.

The county has produced stars of film, stage and television, singers in opera and concert hall, and brass and silver bands, as well as comedians and rock music groups. Distinguished composers hail from Glamorgan, and so do well-known choirs. The art schools of the county turn out artists in stained glass, painting and sculpture, and some noted fashion designers. Its universities and colleges educate students from all over the world. The game of bando - akin to hockey - used to be played between neighbouring villages; nowadays soccer and rugby teams have their enthusiastic fans, while Glamorgan cricket club has its passionate followers. The county is proud of the noted athletes, boxers, billiards and snooker players that it has produced.

We start our survey of Glamorgan by touring the Gower peninsula. Then we join the M4 where it crosses the county border at Pontarddulais, and follow the motorway eastwards to the Gwent border, with forays into the industrialised valleys to the north and to the fertile lowlands to the south. Having visited Cardiff, capital city of Wales, where all the exciting developments are still being planned for Cardiff Bay, we rejoin the M4 and leave Glamorgan.

Gower

Llangennith, Burry Holmes Sand Dunes c1950 L224009
There is evidence that this headland was occupied during the
Iron Age. It is thought that one or two stock-rearing families lived
here, with banks and ditches across the neck of the promontory.
At high tide, the headland becomes an island, making it easier to
defend. The priory was attacked by Vikings in 986.

Llangennith, The General Stores and the Church c1965 L224039
According to legend St Kennith was sent down the river Loughor in a coracle, landed on Worm's Head and founded a monastery at Llangennith. Around 1474, a petition to Henry VI was drafted complaining that a priest named Hugh Haddesley and Sir Hugh John, taking advantage of the turmoil caused by the Wars of the Roses, 'have seized on the priory of Llangennith'.

Llanmadog, Cwm Ivy 1937 88004
The 'City of Bristol' foundered on the Llangennith sands in 1840. According to the Cambrian newspaper, 27 people drowned, but pigs and cattle swam ashore and were penned at Cwm Ivy farm. The remains of an Iron Age hill fort (the Bulwark), dating from 700BC-100AD, may be seen on Llanmadog hill. Allegedly a ghost may be seen in Llanmadog churchyard.

Rhosili
Rough Sea c1950 R25082
The magnificent beach at Rhosili, accessible only along narrow
paths, and popular with swimmers and surfers, curves for 3 miles.
The barque 'Helvetia' was wrecked here in 1877. Rhosili village is
enclosed by an ancient field system: strips of land known as
landshares are bounded by low stone walls. Edgar Evans, who died
with Scott at the South Pole, was born at Rhosili.

Cheriton
The Village and the Church 1937 88007
Elizabeth Delabere, heiress of Sir Roger Delabere, Lord of Cheriton and
Llangennith in the time of Edward III, married David Cradoc, a
descendant of Einon ab Collwyn. They had a son, Philip, and his
descendants are the Craddocks of Swansea and Cheriton. Cheriton
church is known locally as 'Gower Cathedral'. Legend has it that a family
quarrel in 1770 resulted in a man's murder, and that subsequently the
vicar was locked inside his church while an outdoor court was held in
the graveyard. Another legend states that certain stones in the gate-post
should never be touched, otherwise the plague will return.

Reynoldston, General View c1960 R276021
There is a pillar stone inscribed with crosses and plaitwork inside the church at Reynoldston. Probably dating from the 10th century, it once stood on a mound near Stout Hall. A round Bronze Age cairn lies nearby, west of King Arthur's stone.

Reynoldston, King Arthur's Stone c1955 R276060
This marks a megalithic burial chamber from the New Stone Age, which makes the monument at least 4,000 years old. One legend states that it was a pebble from King Arthur's shoe, another that the stone was split by the king using his sword, Excalibur. St David split the stone in order to prove that it was not a sacred stone, according to another tale, and yet another states that on midsummer's eve the stone goes to the Burry river to drink.

Port Eynon, The Lifeboat Memorial 1937 88167
The marble memorial reminds us of an event in 1916: the lifeboat was called out to the SS 'Dunvegan', which was in danger off Pennard in a westerly gale, and three of the lifeboat crew lost their lives. After this, the lifeboat station was closed; the building now houses a Youth Hostel. Two miles west of Port Eynon is Goat's Hole cave where 'The Red Lady of Paviland' was discovered in 1823 by Dean Buckland. It subsequently turned out that what the Dean had found was the remains of a man, and were up to a hundred thousand years old.

Llanrhidian, The Village 1937 87985
There are records of a mill at Llanrhidian in 1375. Weobley castle is nearby. During spring and autumn, the ponies on Llanrhidian marsh may be seen standing up to their necks in the tide. They can drink salt water, and can cross to Whitford burrows, where the rare fen orchid grows.

Pennard, The Castle 1893 32760
Pennard Castle stands on the eastern shore of Pennard Pill, overlooking Three Cliffs Bay. Built in the 12th century, it was abandoned in the 14th century because of sand encroachment. It appears that Minchin Hole cave in the cliffs at Pennard was occupied during the Iron-Age, and also in Roman and medieval times. Bronze brooches and silver coins have been found there. The poet Vernon Watkins (1907-1967) lived at Pennard.

▼ **Penrice, The Castle, the Tower Lodge 1910** 62593
In the 1770s, Thomas Mansel Talbot, with his architect Anthony Keck, built himself a new castle at Penrice. The four-storeyed house in Bath stone boasted a lavish interior adorned with marble and mahogany and containing Dutch and Italian paintings. Trees were planted, and gardens were landscaped. Herons came to the large artificial lake, and the Penrice heronry became well known.

▼ **Oxwich, The Post Office c1955** 038016
Winding narrow sunken lanes abound in Gower, and one of them leads from the village to Oxwich bay. The 12th-century church, St Illtud's, has a recess in its north wall known locally as the Dolamur's hole, and naughty children were threatened with being thrown into it. The old rectory that stood between the church and the sea was washed away, and in 1789 a new rectory (now a hotel) was built.

▲ **Penrice
The Village 1937** 87981
Early in the 12th century, a group of Normans led by Henry de Beaumont, Earl of Warwick, founded the Marcher Lordship of Gower. A small earth and timber castle, mentioned in a charter of 1306, was built at Penrice. In 1410 the land passed to the Mansels, who later acquired Margam Abbey.

◀ **Oxwich**
The View from the Church 1935 038010
The freshwater marshes at Oxwich, which are formed by rivers that have been held back by sand dunes, are national Nature Reserves under the jurisdiction of the Nature Conservancy Council. In 1956 they became the first Area of Outstanding Natural Beauty to be recognised in Britain. John Wesley preached at Oxwich church.

**Oxwich
The Castle 1910**
62599
The original house on
this headland, which
was built by Philip
Mansel, was
demolished when Sir
Rice Mansel built a
comfortable manor
house on the site in the
16th century. His son
Edward, when his father
had moved to Margam
Abbey, brought Oxwich
castle up to date with a
long gallery and great
windows. We can see
the remains of the
circular dovecote on
the left of the
photograph.

◄ **Bishopston
The Church 1893** 32750
St Teilo's church in
Bishopston remained the
property of the Bishopric of
Llandaff for many years after
other Gower churches had
moved to the diocese of St
David's. The church has two
bells dated 1713 and 1714.
In the 17th century, Isaac
Hamon of Bishopston wrote
about the geology, natural
history and the people of
Gower. Laver bread from
Bishopston is sold in
Swansea market.

◄ **Parkmill, The Village 1893** 32756
At Parkmill we can see the earth bank or pale, with its wall and inside ditch, which marks the boundary of the deer park known as Park le Breos. The medieval deer-park was divided into three farms. Parc le Breos House now offers holiday accommodation with horse-riding, cycling and walking in 70 acres of deciduous woodland. The Gower Heritage Centre in Parkmill village has the 12th-century water mill at its centre. The mill outbuildings have been converted into craft workshops where an artist, a potter, a blacksmith, a jeweller, a wheelwright, a mason and a carpenter may be seen at work.

▼ **Newton**
The Village 1893 32742
The village of Newton has seen many changes since this photograph, with a cow being milked at the roadside, was taken. Less than a mile west of Oystermouth, the village stands in the centre of an area of long narrow fields derived from the enclosed strips of an early medieval open field settlement.

◄ **Parkmill**
The Gower Hotel 1910 62589
A traveller in 1861 wrote: 'The resting place is a neat and pleasant inn, the Gower Inn, where good sitting and sleeping rooms may be obtained'. In the past rents were collected here, and in the 21st century, the inn is still popular. A short walk away a memorial stone pinpoints the site of the first Baptist Church in Wales, 1649-1660. The founder, John Miles, and his followers emigrated to America in 1663 and founded a Baptist chapel in Swansea, Massachusetts. The mock-Gothic school house is now a Girl Guides centre. Corn is still ground at the mill that gave the village its name.

Newton, The Village 1910 62582
J P Jones ran the village shop in 1910. Open gutters had still not
been done away with. In 1900 Harold Williams, vicar of
Oystermouth, formed a building committee to erect a new church
at Newton. In the same year foundations were being dug, and the
church was consecrated by Bishop Lloyd of Swansea on 19
November 1903. Newton remained part of the parish of
Oystermouth until 1933, when it became a separate parish.

Gower, Threecliff Bay 1893 32758
This bay can be reached only by walking the cliff-top footpath. The currents are treacherous to swimmers, but the area is popular with abseilers and paragliders. In 1917 a cargo of French wine was swept ashore; it was soon disposed of by the locals, some of whom, reportedly, did not arrive home until later next day.

Caswell Bay 1901 47964
Caswell and Langland bays, being nearer to Swansea, are always the busiest in Gower. Before motoring became universal, families from Swansea used to take the Mumbles train to Oystermouth and walk with children and push-chairs, kettles and picnic provisions to their favourite beach for the day.

**Langlands Bay
The Bathing Beach
1893** 32745
An idyllic beach for
children, and popular
with bathers in 1893,
Langlands is as popular
as ever in the 21st
century. In the eastern
end of the bay, known
as Rotherslade, a bone
cave was discovered.
The remains are in
Swansea museum, and
the cave - Rothers Tor
Cave - has been filled in.

**Langland
The Convalescent
Home 1925** 77412
Langland Bay House
was built in the mid
19th century for a
member of the
Crawshay family; the
Crawshays were
ironmasters of Cyfarthfa
Castle, Merthyr. For
many years it has been
used as a hotel and as a
convalescent home.

Oystermouth
The Cemetery 1899 43673

This cemetery contains the graves of many shipwrecked sailors. One of them is Samuel Dunstone, who drowned aged 33 when his ship the 'Cornish Diamond' was wrecked on Mixon sands on the 20th of April 1871, and all hands perished. Thomas Bowdler was buried in this churchyard in 1835. He had written expurgated versions of the works of Shakespeare, and it is from his name that the word 'bowdlerise' is derived. In 1872, in his diary, Kilvert described Oystermouth castle standing nobly on a hill, and the great fleet of oyster boats in the bay. The church of All Saints is said to have been built on the site of a Roman villa. Fragments of paving that were unearthed in 1860 are now embedded in a slate tablet on its west wall. Among the rubble brought back as ballast in one of Swansea's copper barques in 1865 were bells from the Jesuit church of La Compania, Santiago, Chile. Three of the bells, with Spanish inscriptions, are in Oystermouth church, and a fourth one is in Christchurch, Carmarthen.

Mumbles
Oystermouth Castle 1893 32737
William de Londres built a timber castle at Oystermouth. When it
was attacked and burnt by Gruffydd ap Rhys in 1106, it is said that
William 'through fear of Gruffydd, left his castle and all his cattle
and all his wealth'. The castle was rebuilt in stone in the 14th
century, and Alina, heiress of William de Breose, lived there.

**Mumbles
The Pier 1898** 40925
The Mumbles railway
began as a tramroad
authorised by an Act of
Parliament in 1804; it
carried limestone and
coal until one of the
original shareholders,
Benjamin French, used
a horse-drawn wagon to
carry passengers on it,
thus making it the first
passenger railway
service in the world. It
became very popular in
1879 when steam
power was introduced,
and it was extended to
Mumbles Pier in 1898.

Mumbles, The Lighthouse 1893 32731
The original lighthouse, built in 1793, had a coal-fired beacon, later, oil and then gas were used. Nowadays a solar-powered 100-watt quartz iodine electric lamp provides the light. Tradition says that the pirate Bob kept his plunder in the large sea cave at the end of the island. The pirate John Avery was hanged near here in 1731.

Mumbles, The Promenade 1898 40927
With the Mumbles Railway carrying as many as 40,000 passengers on a bank holiday, the village prospered.
The rail system was electrified in 1929, and the railway was closed in 1960. Now cyclists and walkers use the track, which has been paved to make a popular pathway from Swansea marina and along the length of Swansea bay.

Gowerton, Sterry Road c1955 G152011
Sterry Road was named after an industrialist from Croydon, Alfred Sterry. He came here in 1855, and in 1858 he sank the Gorwydd colliery. He then built a battery of coke ovens near the Great Western Railway. Coal was brought here from his own colliery, and also from other nearby pits over their own tramroads, to be processed into coke which was sold to works in Swansea and Llanelli. Ernest Jones, psychoanalyst and friend and disciple of Freud, and an early member of Plaid Cymru, was born in Gowerton.

Gowerton, Sterry Road c1955 G152003
In this view we are looking towards the level crossing and Dunraven Terrace. The signals and level crossing gates were operated from the signal box. After the line from Swansea to Pontarddulais was closed in 1965, the gates, signals and footbridge were removed.

▼ **Pontarddulais, Hermon Square c1955** P165043

The traffic system has been altered since the Hermon Methodist chapel was built in 1893. Pontarddulais was involved in the activities of the Rebecca rioters in the 19th century. An aged female gatekeeper was killed in 1843 at nearby Hendy, resulting in some rioters being transported to Van Dieman's land. By an act of 1844 the tolls on lime were reduced by half, and all the turnpike trusts within each shire in South Wales were amalgamated.

▼ **Pontarddulais, The Viaduct c1955** P165004

Known locally as The Eleven Arches, this viaduct is still in use, but nowadays carries only freight.

▲ **Gorseinon, The Square 1936** 87814

The Brynlliw Colliery was established in Gorseinon in 1908 to work the anthracite or high quality dry steam coal of the Swansea Six-feet seam, and production was increased when the National Coal Board introduced horizon mining. In 1899 the Bryngwyn Steelworks opened, and in 1908 six sheet mills and a galvanising plant were added. Tinworks were opened at Grovesend, Gorseinon in 1886. Richard Thomas and Co bought it in 1923.

West Glamorgan

◀ **Pontlliw**
Gwynn's Service Station 1937 87906
The growth of road traffic gave rise to new petrol service stations. Bassett's bus company, Gorseinon, bought William Rees's carpenter's workshop on this site and opened the petrol station in the 1930s. It was run by Mr Gwynn and his son, Marcel. They had an ornamental pool in front of their premises, and on one occasion they caught three fox-cubs near the pool which they kept in their shed, a popular local attraction. Marcel joined the RAF and lost his life during the war. Bassett's sold the business to Ron Day; then it was taken over by Alun and Roger Davies, and in 1986 was acquired by Glenn Murray, who still runs the business.

Swansea, High Street 1899 43975
The High Street, leading to the railway station (which opened in 1850, providing access to London and other parts of the country), was thriving in the decades before the First World War. It contained department stores, hotels, furniture shops and shoe shops, and it was noisy with horse-drawn vehicles and advertisement-adorned trams. In 1821 Swansea became the first place in Wales to illuminate its streets with gas lighting. Much of the town was destroyed by bombs in World War II, and the High Street changed in character. Lately some buildings around the castle have been demolished, and the ruins remind us of the turbulent times when many Glamorgan men fought with Owain Glyndwr in his attacks on Swansea castle.

◄ Swansea, High Street 1893 32720

Swansea, being a port, and having plentiful supplies of coal available, was ideally placed for the growth of the copper industry. Its population in 1801 stood at 6,000, but by 1911 it had increased to 115,000. The town gained city-status in 1969. A new marina has been constructed in the dock area along with a maritime museum, the Dylan Thomas centre, hotels and apartments. A statue in the marina honours John Henry Vivian MP, a copper smelter; he had come to Swansea from Cornwall, and his family became the wealthiest and most powerful in the town. The family lived at Singleton Abbey. In 1893 Sir Henry Hussey Vivian was granted the title of Lord Swansea. His estate was acquired by the Local Authority after the First World War.

▼ Swansea
The General and Eye Hospital 1893 32722

The London architect Alexander Graham's design for the Swansea General and Eye Hospital was approved by Florence Nightingale. It opened in 1864. Most of it has been demolished, but the main admission block, with its slim clock cupola, still stands. Singleton Hospital was built in 1960.

◄ Swansea
The South Dock 1906 54952

The South Dock was opened in 1859 when copper-smelting and tinplate manufacture were major industries in Swansea. At this time, about 35 Swansea vessels were engaged in the copper-ore trade, sailing regularly to South America. Ship building and repairing gave work to many, and Swansea came sixth in the list of British ship-owning ports. John Vivian opened the first of his copper smelting furnaces at Hafod, Swansea in 1810. In 1838 work began at Upper Bank Copperworks which led to the invention of Muntz Metal, or Yellow Metal. An alloy of zinc and copper, it was used from 1842 onwards for sheathing the bottoms of ships.

Swansea
The Sands 1925 77376
The beach has always been popular with Swansea residents,
especially the area known as 'the slip' near Victoria Park and
County Hall. The Mumbles railway that ran along its length has now
given way to a promenade and cycle path.

Morriston, Woodfield Street c1955 M179017

The Morris family founded Morriston. Robert Morris (1700-1768), with two others, bought Llangyfelach copper works at Landore, and later the Fforest copper works. He also owned brass wire mills and collieries, and in 1728 he bought Mackworth's Colliery, Treboeth. John Morris (1745-1819) later became Sir John Morris. The family home was at Clasemont. In his book published in 1903, Charles Wilkins refers to the large number of girls and women employed at Morriston tinplate works. 'This girl-woman had a leather apron and two leather gloves and the ease with which she seized upon a plate, struck it a blow, and ripped it into sheets, was wonderful. Layer after layer came off just like stripping one vegetable layer from another instead of tough steel'.

Morriston, Woodfield Street c1955 M179033

Sir John Morris (1745-1819) of Clasemont continued his father's work. He conceived the idea for a 'company housing scheme', and built a castellated mansion with an inner quadrangle with dwellings for a tailor, a shoemaker and 40 families. In 1768 he laid the foundations of Morriston along with a church and a chapel. The architect was the bridge builder, William Edwards. He added a tower to the chapel, an unusual feature.

Llansamlet
Heol Las 1938 88275
Coal-pits were sunk around Llansamlet in 1798. The south-westerly prevailing winds meant
that Llansamlet and Bonymaen were the districts worst affected by air pollution from the metal
industries. The consequences were described by Dr Thomas Williams, stating that the surface
of the land north and north-east of the town looked as if it was scorched. All that could be
seen was stones, red gravel, and black slag, and the ground was practically denuded of
vegetation as a result of sulphurous copper smoke. All the water was stagnant and destitute of
pond life. Some departments of University College, Swansea combined to gather information
on the Lower Swansea valley, and published their report in 1966. They found acorns in the
peat in Llansamlet, and deduced that the area had once been forested but the continuous air
pollution had killed the trees. In 1961 the ruins of Llansamlet Chemical Works were
demolished with the help of members of the Territorial Army, who used several small
explosive charges. In 1964 health visitors carried out a house-to-house census to test the lung
function of women living in the area. In comparison with women living in the Vale of
Glamorgan, there was a considerably higher incidence of chronic bronchitis in Llansamlet.

Clungwyn Falls
The Middle Fall 1898 40939
Over the years, the picturesque waterfalls of the Neath valley have
yielded stones for building and power for industries, as well as
water for domestic use. The Clungwyn falls of the Mellte river are
featured in the folk tales of the area. The tales relate how the 'ceffyl-
dwr' - a frisky snow-white horse - would emerge from the foaming
cascade and tempt the weary traveller to mount him. Sometimes he
would then carry them to safety. But at other times he would fly
over hills and valleys and dump the poor traveller many miles away
before slowly disappearing into a cloud.

▼ Cilybebyll, The Lodge 1937 88149

Neath Ultra and Cilybebyll passed from Neath Abbey to Gilbert de Clare in 1269. Later they were owned by the crown, and then by the Earls of Pembroke. By 1715 Sir Humphrey Mackworth, who restarted the copper industry in Neath, had gained possession of them. In 1891, Jacob Beach, a gamekeeper, lived in this thatched lodge built in the shape of a kraal. It caught fire in the 1960s and has now been modernised.

▼ Rhydyfro, Commercial Road 1938 88364

Gilbertson and Company bought the corn mill at Rhydyfro because they feared that it robbed the tinplate works of water. Gilbertson had purchased the tinplate works at Pontardawe and Trebanos, and was living at Ynysderw House by 1861. A young woman named Eliza James from Rhydyfro emigrated to Australia in 1882. She was praised in the Sydney newspapers for her singing, and was named 'Eos Rhydyfro'. She visited the Eisteddfod in London in 1909, and was made a member of the Gorsedd before returning to Australia.

▲ Pontardawe General View c1965

P183016

The stone bridge that gives the town its name was built by the famous William Edwards around 1760. Little remains today of the tinplate works, the steel works, the coal mines, the chemical works, the pottery, the fire-clay works, the woollen mills, the corn mills, the foundry and the gas-works that brought employment to the town, though new factories came to the Alloy Industrial Estate in 1965.

◄ **Gwaun-cae-Gurwen**
Church Street c1955 G153007
The Gwaun-cae-Gurwen Colliery Co Ltd
employed 1,800 men. Coal from the
colliery won a series of awards at
continental trade exhibitions from the
1880s onwards. During the 1820s, new
roads were being built in Glamorgan.
The road over the open common at
Gwaun-cae-Gurwen was built by Lord
Dynevor with a loan from the Exchequer
Loans Commissioner, and later it was
taken over by the Neath Trust. The
miners' silver band was well known
when anthracite coal was mined at
Gwaun-cae-Gurwen; it is still going
strong today, despite the effects of pit
closures. The actress Sian Phillips was
born in Gwaun-cae-Gurwen.

**Port Talbot
Station Road c1955**
P139021
The new borough of
Port Talbot came into
existence in 1921 from
the amalgamation of
Aberafan, Baglan, Bryn,
Taibach, Oakwood,
Margam and Cwmafan.
In that year the
population stood at
40,027. Its name is
derived from Port Talbot
Docks, which were
owned by the Mansel
Talbot family of
Margam.

▼ Port Talbot, The M4 Motorway c1966 P139063

As the town stands on a narrow strip of land between the mountains and the sea, the management of road traffic in Port Talbot was not easy. There was no room for a bypass, so the M4 motorway, which opened in 1966, was built above the town's roofs; Capel Moriah, Vivian Square and Carmarthen Row were demolished in the process. Aberafan shopping centre, visible from the motorway, was opened by the Princess Royal in 1976, and the new Civic Centre in 1989.

▼ Aberavon, The Jersey Beach Hotel c1965 A95001

The improvement in road conditions as well as the coming of the railway opened up Aberavon beach to visitors. Many stayed at the Jersey Beach Hotel, and many arrived for the day by excursion trains. There were bathing machines, refreshment kiosks, donkey rides and swingboats, and people could watch the steamboats steaming in to Port Talbot Docks.

▲ Margam
The Castle, the North Front 1938 88261
Margam Castle was built for 'Britain's wealthiest commoner', Christopher Rice Mansel Talbot, who was MP for Glamorgan for 60 years. It had 41 bedrooms, and it needed more than 100 servants to run it. The hall and the octagonal tower have been restored and opened to visitors.

◀ **Briton Ferry**
The Incline c1950
B398013
The South Wales Mineral
Railway line, designed by
Brunel, was opened for
traffic in 1861. After leaving
Briton Ferry, the trucks had
to be pulled up to the top of
the hill by a powerful rope.
When the South Wales
Mineral Railway was
absorbed by the Port Talbot
Railway, this portion of the
line fell into disuse.

Neath, The Abbey 1893 32725A
Part of the main gateway of the Cistercian abbey founded in 1130
remains amongst the ruins. Close by are the sites of a Roman
camp and of a Norman castle. After the dissolution in 1539, Sir
Richard Williams converted part of the abbey into a mansion. Later
it was used as a copper smelting works, and in the 1950s it was a
popular venue for stock car racing.

Neath, St David's Church 1898 40946

According to legend, an underground passage in which a monster guarded a treasure chest ran from Neath castle to Neath Abbey. But a subsidence in the tramway road at the main entrance to Victoria Gardens revealed only colliery roadways. St David's church was built for the English congregation in 1866. The tower, 152 feet high, is named the Victoria Tower after the Vaughan family of Rheola. William Vaughan chaired the general meeting of the Glamorgan Society that met in the Ship and Castle Inn in Neath in 1816. The society gave prizes for ploughing, and also for hoeing by oxen and by horses. William Vaughan introduced Cheviot sheep to the area, and initiated improvements in agriculture in the Vale of Neath.

Glyn Neath, Aberpergwm Church c1955 G149011

This church - composed of chancel, nave, porch and turret with one bell - stands in the midst of fields. Parish stocks at the gate entrance survived until 1840. There is a tablet inside the church commemorating David Nicholas, bard in residence at Aberpergwm Mansion. Maria Jane Williams of Aberpergwm, with the encouragement of Lady Llanover, published her volume of Welsh folk songs in 1844.

Resolven, The Bridge c1965 R275013
Coal was carried on the Cwm Clydach tramroad over this bridge to the wharf on the Vale of Neath canal. When the railway superseded the canal, the bridge was adapted for road traffic. A 'New Bridge' in this area is marked on Kitchin's map of 1754, but heavier vehicles used to cross the river at a nearby ford.

Glyncorrwg, The Town 1938 88634
Although the South Wales Mineral Line was supposed to carry goods only, passengers were carried in the guard's van between Neath and Glyncorrwg over a period of forty years. David Nicholas was a teacher at Glyncorrwg in 1742 before his appointment as bard of Aberpergwm Mansion.

Mid and South Glamorgan

Pontypridd, The Old Bridge c1965 P716040

A local mason, William Edwards, built this 140ft single arch bridge over the river Taff in 1755. His two earlier attempts had been unsuccessful, but he reduced the weight of the structure by piercing 3 cylindrical holes in each of the spandrels and achieved his objective. He went on to build bridges in other locations. Nearby is a heritage centre with mementoes of the composers of the Welsh National Anthem and of Tom Jones and Stuart Burrows.

Abertridwr, The Square c1965 A195024

Workmen's Institutes played an important part in the lives of the miners. They held libraries and evening classes, snooker and billiards were played there, and concerts and eisteddfodau took place there. The Institutes provided an alternative to the public house as a place for socialising.

**Pontypridd
Market Street 1899**
43605
The colliery owners at
Pontypridd, such as
Gethin, Insoles, Coffin
and others, found that
the transport available
was insufficient for
delivering good steam
coal to their customers.
The steam engine
designed by Trevithick
was too heavy for the
tramlines, so the Taff
Vale Railway received
royal assent in 1836.
Isambard Kingdom
Brunel surveyed and
planned the route.
Pontypridd was the
biggest junction of the
system, with a train
passing every two
minutes.

Ynyshir, General View c1965 Y33001
James Thomas (1817-1901) sank Ynyshir and Standard collieries. His grandson and heir, William James Thomas (1867-1945), donated £90,000 for establishing the Welsh National School of Medicine. He was treasurer of Cardiff Royal Infirmary, and built the village of TreThomas. In 1919 King George V conferred the baronetcy of Ynyshir on him.

Treorchy, Station Road c1965 T197050
The Park and Dare Workmen's Hall (left) was opened in 1913. The Park and Dare Band, supported by local artistes, advertised a Grand Concert to be held there on 6 February 1947, to celebrate the nationalisation of the coal industry.

Treherbert, The Llyn and the Horse Shoe Bend c1955 T196020

The Marquis of Bute named Treherbert in memory of his ancestors, the Earls of Pembroke. In 1855 the first load of coal left Bute Merthyr pit in Treherbert, the 4ft mine having been reached at the depth of 115 metres. Brickworks that gave employment to a considerable number of girls were established in 1858. Early in the 1860s the Bute Trustees suggested to their co-landowners that a main valley road laid down to a width of 50 feet should be built from Treherbert to Pontypridd; they then went ahead and constructed the road as far as Treorchy. There were 3 horse-omnibus services daily from Treherbert to Ystrad in the late 1870s, and in 1908 the first electric tramcar was in use.

Tonypandy, Clydach Street c1955 T192008

The town's name is derived from the fulling mill built there in 1738. The rope-worked incline at Pwllyrhebog near Tonypandy was worked by specially-designed engines right up to 1951. The lift at Tonypandy station was unique in that it worked from the up platform to street level, and was hydraulically worked by using water from the nearby river.

Aberdare, The Park 1937 87888

Aberdare park was opened in 1869. The statue is of Sir William Thomas Lewis, Baron Merthyr of Senghenydd, who had a hand in the planning of the park. The splendid iron gates and railings remind us that this was an iron town. International cyclists practised regularly in the park, and during the 1926 strike, competitions for brass bands were held there. Now it has a boating lake with rowing boats and pedaloes for hire. Aberdare was the first district in Wales to provide an open-air school for delicate and handicapped children.

Aberdare, The Cenotaph 1937 87890

Armistice Day services are held annually at the cenotaph in Aberdare. A more ornate statue stands in Victoria Square. It depicts 'Caradog' (Griffith Rhys Jones, 1834-1897). He conducted the massed choir, with members from all parts of South Wales, that won 1st prize at the Crystal Palace in 1873 and 1874. The silver cup that they brought home in triumph is now at Aberystwyth University museum. When the National Eisteddfod was held in Aberdare in 1956, police diverted traffic away from the square while a crowd of about 2,000 sang near Caradog's statue. Led by Tawe Griffiths, they sang until 2.00am. The first Co-op shop opened in Cwmbach, Aberdare in 1860.

Mountain Ash, General View 1938 88695
David Williams, son of a tenant farmer, sank Duffryn pit in 1850. John Nixon (1815-1899) began sinking the Navigation pit in 1855. He bought the Deep Duffryn mine from David Williams for £42,000 in 1856, and he introduced new methods of ventilation. His portrait may be seen in the east window of St Margaret's church, Caegarw. Between the two wars the Miners' Welfare Committee built bath houses for their workers. J H Forshaw designed one in reinforced concrete for the Cwm Cynon Colliery, Mountain Ash.

Mountain Ash, The War Memorial 1938 88700
The memorial monument erected in Mountain Ash after the first world war bears this message: 'Sons of this town and district, Let this be said that you who live are worthy of your dead. These gave their lives that you may live, may reap a richer harvest ere you fall asleep'. Penrhiwceiber children's choir travelled widely in South Wales raising money for the miners during the 1926 strike.

◄ Pyle
Maudlam Church and the
Angel Hotel 1938 87730A
This church is dedicated to
St Mary Magdalen:
Maudlam is a corrupted
form of Magdalen. The
original church was in the
village of Kenfig, near
Fitzhammon's castle. About
the year 1300 a series of
typhoon-like storms hit the
area, and the village and
most of the church were
buried in sand. The Norman
font, patterned with fish
scales, from the buried
church was installed in
St Mary Magdalen's church.

◄ Bridgend
Dunraven Place 1898 41199

In 1632 the first cattle market was held in Dunraven Place. The Wyndham Arms, a Grade II listed building, used to be an important coaching inn. The Victorian clock opposite the inn remains an object of interest. The National Provincial Bank commenced business in Bridgend in 1835. There is a plaque in Bridgend library to honour Dr Richard Price of Tynton Farm in the Garw valley. He voiced his support for the rebels in the American War of Independence, and had a hand in the drafting of the American Declaration of Independence. He also influenced the beginning of life insurance and pension schemes. He was granted an honorary degree from Yale University in 1781.

▼ Penrhiwceiber
Penrhiwceiber Road
c1955 P224002

For many years, Mountain Ash and Penrhiwceiber organised a New Year's Eve race to honour the memory of Guto Nyth Bran (Griffith Morgan), who was said to have run 12 miles in 53 minutes. His gravestone at St Gwynno's church states that he died in 1737 aged 37.

◄ Abercynon
The Clock Tower c1955
A191046

In earlier times, Abercynon was called Navigation House. Coal was transported using horse-drawn trams on tramways to the Glamorganshire canal at Pontypridd for shipment to Cardiff Docks. Iron products from the iron works at Dowlais and Merthyr also depended on the tramways. In 1804 Richard Trevithick designed a steam engine and, for a bet, drove it down the Merthyr tramroad to Abercynon.

Bridgend, Parc Gwyllt Hospital 1899 43357

The original medieval settlement grew up around the crossing point on the river Ogmore which was used by pilgrims to St David's. The old bridge, built in 1425, was damaged by flood in 1775 and then rebuilt. It is now a Grade 2 listed structure. In 1851 the railway came to Bridgend, and another 2 railways opened in 1892. The remains of the Norman castle overlook the town.

Bridgend, Caroline Street 1938 88304

This street is named after Caroline, Countess of Dunraven. She initiated the building of the Randall memorial drinking fountain in the town to commemorate John Randall, who managed her estates for 33 years. The old market bell is on display at the entrance to the covered market. The Bridgend Industrial Estate now occupies the site on which the Royal Ordnance Factory once stood during the last war. At its busiest time, it gave employment to 37,000 people. The Remploy factory, opened in 1946, employed disabled people; some travelled to work from Maesteg, Pontycymmer and Ogmore Vale, and some worked from home. Now the major employers include Sony, Ford and Bauer Pharmaceuticals.

Merthyr Mawr
The Post Office 1937 87881
The Vale of Glamorgan used to grow a great deal of corn,
ensuring ample straw for thatching, and the village of Merthyr
Mawr is entirely made up of thatched houses. The oldest of
these dates back to the 14th century. A medieval bridge over
the Ogwr has holes in its sides where sheep were driven into
the river to be dipped. There are pre-Conquest memorials at the
ruined Oratory nearby. Sand dunes hide prehistoric remains.

◄ **Merthyr Mawr**
The Old Church School
1937 87884
The climbing plant on the wall
has been as firmly disciplined
as were the former pupils
who attended this school. The
sand dunes of Merthyr Mawr
Warren - a site of Special
Scientific Interest - are among
the highest in Europe, and
contain a rich variety of plants
and animals. Candleston
Castle, a 15th-century
fortified manor house, was
inhabited by the Cantelupe
family. Wind-blown sand
covered the small settlement
around it.

Blaengwynfi
Western Colliery 1938 88714

Houses for the colliers were built around the pit which dominated their lives. The sound of the hooter at set times signalled the end of shifts, but when it sounded at an unusual time, it conveyed news of a pit accident. Since 1977 the Afan Burrough has undertaken reclamation works at the sites of the Avon and Scatton colliery and of the disused railway. They felt that the crumbling buildings and steeply sloping pits were apt to be used as playgrounds by local children, putting their safety at risk, and that their removal would be of considerable benefit to the communities of the upper Afan valley.

Bridgend
Ogmore Castle 1898
41216

There are many stories told about these stepping stones over the river Ogmore. According to one, the heiress of Ogmore Castle had them set there so that her lover could visit her more easily. Another tale states that the stones themselves moved down from rougher water further up river.

Ewenny
Bridgend Pottery
1937 87908

Ewenny pottery was established in 1801, and has been owned by the Jenkins family ever since. One of the older kilns has been reconstructed at the National Folk Museum, St Fagans. A Benedictine priory was built here on the site of an earlier church by monks from Gloucester cathedral. The nave still forms part of the parish church.

▼ **Kenfig, The Square 1966** K92005
Kenfig Pool, held back by sand dunes, is the largest freshwater lake in Glamorgan.
The town of Kenfig on a site nearby was covered by sand in a series of gales in the
14th century. After a final gale in the 16th century, that town was abandoned and
another was developed. Now the pool forms part of a Nature Reserve. It is alleged
that the sound of church bells may still be heard here.

▼ **Bridgend, An Old Cottage and the Stepping Stones 1937** 87993
Some maintain that the stepping stones were set in place for funeral processions at
a time when coffins had to be carried for long distances. Now they are enjoyed by
visitors, and make a fine excuse for a snapshot. A little further down the river are
the remnants of a medieval fish weir.

▲ **Ogmore By Sea
The Dunes and the
River c1955** 072098
The name Ogmore is
derived from the Welsh
words eog (salmon) and
môr (sea or expanse of
water.)

**Ogmore By Sea
The River c1955** 072124
This part of the coast, with its sand dunes and hidden valleys, was the haunt of smugglers and difficult to control. One customs officer wrote that a vessel had unloaded a large consignment of coffee, cocoa and sugar at Newton. 'The country people are outrageous and threaten our very lives', he wrote. He was also angry that the smuggler had already landed his quota of rum at Mumbles.

◄ **Newton**
The Village c1950
N123008
The Norman church of
St John the Baptist at
Newton has a defensive
tower, as is common in
coastal regions.
Dinosaur footprints from
the late Triassic period
were found near Newton
church in 1878. They
are now in the National
Museum, Cardiff, and a
plaster cast of the slab
may be seen at
Porthcawl museum.

◄ **Porthcawl**
John Street 1901 47941
Porthcawl's growth is due to the opening of the Docks in 1867, and the expansion of the coal trade. When more sheltered deep water docks opened in Barry and Port Talbot, Porthcawl's trade dwindled. In 1943, the inner basin was infilled with waste from collieries at Aberkenfig, and it is now a car-park known as Salt Lake.

▼ **Porthcawl**
John Street 1938 88461
From the 1930s Porthcawl developed as a seaside resort. Coney Beach fairground was built on an old tip where ballast from ships had been dumped. Ice cream parlours, restaurants and cafes catered for visitors, and the Esplanade and the Royal Porthcawl Golf Club added to Porthcawl's popularity. The Miners' Eisteddfod was held at the Pavilion each October.

◄ **Newton**
Beach Bungalows c1950 N123011
Newton village was founded by Richard de Cardiff in the 12th century. It became a thriving port exporting wheat, oats and knitted stockings. The Norman Fitzhammon built a castle at Kenfig, and one of his underlings, Baron de Sturmi, built a motte and bailey at Stormy Down (hence its name). With the inclusion of Ogmore castle, built by William de Londres, these Normans had created what was described in deeds as 'Novau Villam in Margam', 'a new town'. The town of Kenfig would probably have engulfed Newton and Nottage, but it itself was engulfed by sand.

Nottage 1938 88468
According to some historians, this was the site of an early Celtic settlement; its original name was Llanddewi. There is a holy well on the outskirts where St David or one of his hermit saints may have had a cell in the 5th century. When the railway tunnel was being built, many human bones were found. The Vikings used Nottage as a trading post. What is thought to have been a Viking grave was unearthed in 1846. It contained an urn containing human remains which had been burned with a mixture of earth and brushwood, said to be typical of Scandinavian custom. Pirates infested the Bristol Channel even as late as Elizabeth I's time. Newton Nottage church had a fortified roof for protection.

Nottage, West Road c1955 N124011
Nottage, older than Porthcawl, dates back to pre-Norman times. In one of the walls surrounding the village green there is a stone inscribed with a fleur de lys. The village green was given to the community by the Nottage Court Estate in 1983.

Maesteg, Commercial Street c1955 M210012
Iron was the main industry in Maesteg for 50 years, but by 1887 the last furnace had closed. Demand for steam coal caused collieries to be developed, and over a million tons of coal were mined annually. Working people now work in modern industrial estates, or commute to adjoining towns.

Maesteg, The Town Hall and the War Memorial c1955 M210003
The Town Hall in the centre of Maesteg, built by the people of Llynfi valley, is now a popular venue for the arts, with exhibitions, a cinema and live entertainment. Here dinners and wedding celebrations can be held. The town was formed around the Maesteg ironworks in the late 1820s, and later the Llynfi Ironworks came into being. Iron ore and coal were extracted from the surrounding hills. The first coal-cutting machinery to be used in Wales (as far as is known) came into operation at Garth colliery, Maesteg, in 1870.

Llangynwyd, Cefn-Ydfa, Ann Thomas's Memorial 1937 87861
Cefn Ydfa Manor, now being restored, was the home of Ann Thomas, the 'Maid of Cefn Ydfa', who fell in love with handsome poet Wil Hopkyn, a tiler and plasterer by trade. Her ambitious mother contrived marriage for her daughter with Anthony Maddock, only to see Ann sink into depression and eventually die in Wil Hopkyn's arms.

Nantymoel, General View c1955 N121014
The Western Colliery was sunk in Nantymoel by David Davies of the Ocean Coal Company. The colliery had over 8 miles of underground roadway, with 5 miles of high-speed conveyors. It closed in January 1984. The Wyndham Colliery was sunk in 1865 by James Brogden; it was sold to North, and then bought by Cory Brothers in 1906 and by Powell Duffryn in 1942. Because of the narrowness of the valleys, houses had to be built in terraces. At first there was overcrowding as workers moved in to work at the mines.

Pontycymmer, Oxford Street c1955 P227010
Just west of Pontycymmer, the Garw Fechan Woodland Park has been created in an area once scarred by mining.
Woodpeckers, buzzards and ravens have settled there, and tourists walking the marked pathways can find modern
sculptures placed among the trees.

Gilfach Goch, Looking up the Valley c1955 G177027
Evan Evans, a monoglot Welshman, started coal mining here during the latter part of the 19th century. A farmer in
the Neath valley who had moved to Merthyr, and had worked as a haulier and later a collier, he ran the Six Bells
public house and brewery. In 1862 he opened the Six Bells coal level. He built rows of houses with gardens for his
employees. At the time of his death, 400 workers were employed by him at Dinas Main Colliery. His son,
Christmas Evans, sank 2 deep shafts at Gilfach Goch - the Britannic Merthyr Collieries.

Pencoed, The Square c1960 P222001
Coalpits were sunk in Pencoed, and there was a foundry and a brickworks here as well following the opening of the South Wales railway. In 1862 the National School opened, using church premises, and it was followed by a Board School in 1879, the Pencoed Senior School in 1931 and a comprehensive school in 1973. The Mid Glamorgan College of Agriculture and Horticulture is at Tregroes, former home of the Thomas family.

Abergarw, The Bridge 1938 88339
Some believe that the river's name, 'Garw', is derived from the Welsh word for 'rough', but others think it comes from 'carw', meaning 'deer', that were once common in the area. The Garw stream, once polluted by industry, has profited from the Garw Valley Green Strategy Millennium Project, with local communities working to create pleasant well-signposted paths where coal was once predominant. Bryngarw House, built 1834, is now a conference centre and restaurant set in gardens and parkland.

Tondu, The Junction 1938 88335
Sir Robert Price, who owned a colliery at Bettws, built ironworks at Tondu in the 1820s, and constructed a watercourse and a tramway to connect them. He built his company shop near the tramline, trading in groceries, drapery, footwear, ironmongery, meat and other domestic goods. The iron workers were paid in paper money to be spent in the shop, and sometimes their payment was delayed for eight or nine weeks and they had to run up an account. The workman's debts would be deducted from his wages, and the balance paid to him. The Duffryn, Llynvi and Porthcawl railway, adapted from the tramway, served the ironworks in and around the Llynfi valley. The river Llynfi, part of the Ogmore river system and once heavily polluted, is now clean and supports salmon, herons and otters.

Aberkenfig, Bridgend Road 1938 88337
In 1892 there was an explosion at Park Slip colliery, Tondu, which was owned by North's Navigation Company. Of the 110 men who died, 5 were brothers, members of the Lyddon family of Aberkenfig. Parc Slip is now a nature reserve where rare dragonflies breed. Adjacent to the Sarn Motorway Services, Aberkenfig has seen the tourist industry taking over from the heavy industries of the past. The waste from its coal pits was taken to infill the docks at Porthcawl.

Pontyclun, Cowbridge Road c1955 P176024
Industries established in Pontyclun as a result of the coming of the railway in 1850 included Messrs Noel Ltd's Pipe and Sanitary Works; it exported earthenware utensils to Europe and South America. The tinplate works owned by W H Edwards employed 300 workers, including women and juveniles. According to D J Francis, the women worked from 6.30am to 5.30pm and earned 8s per week. The Royal Sovereign Pencil company came here in 1946.

Cowbridge, The Grammar School c1955 C313007
Sir Edward Stradling of St Donat's Castle had planned the founding of the Grammar School at Cowbridge before his death in 1609, but it was his heir, John Stradling, who brought the plan to fruition. He bought premises and appointed a relative, Walter Stradling, to be the first schoolmaster.

Southerndown, The Post Office 1901 47922

About a mile distant from this solidly-built Post Office stood the castellated mansion of the Earl of Dunraven. Once used as a military hospital, it was demolished in 1968. There is a Heritage Coast Centre for tourists at Southerndown.

Llysworney, Nash Manor 1936 87807

Howell Carne leased the manor from the Bishop of Llandaff in 1432. The Carne family, patrons of Welsh literature, intermarried with other noble families such as the Stradlings. Nash Manor contains a large stone fireplace carved with scenes of men indulging in sword-fights - allegedly members of the Carne and Stradling families.

St Donat's Castle, The Tudor Gardens 1910 62537
In 1961 Atlantic College, a pioneering international school for 6th-formers, was opened at St Donat's Castle. William Randolph Hearst, the newspaper magnate, owned the castle at one time, and entertained movie stars here. It now houses an Arts Centre.

St Donat's Castle c1965 S15008
This was the home of the Stradling family. John Stradling (1563-1637), knighted in 1608, and created a baronet by James I in 1611, was sheriff of Glamorgan on three occasions. He published many books, in 1620 he wrote this verse: 'And in Glamorgan's hilly partes/Coal greatlie doth abound/For goodness and for plenty too/ It's equal ne'er was found'. In 1625 he succeeded Sir Robert Mansel as MP for Glamorgan.

Llantwit Major, The Church 1936 87665
The 13th-century church of St Illtud contains Celtic crosses and inscribed stones. One memorial stone records the death in 1534 of Matthew Voss, aged 129 years. According to local legend, the first church to be built here by Eurgain, daughter of the chieftain Caradog, was destroyed by Irish pirates. St Illtud came from Brittany to settle here in the 6th century, and started the first university.

St Athan, The Village c1955 S435068
In 1744 Edward Williams and Ann Matthew were married in the church of St Athan, their son was Iolo Morgannwg. He was apprenticed to a stone-mason, and an example of his work when he was aged 20 can be seen on the tombstone of the Spencer family in the church. St Athan aerodrome was built during the Second World War, and many new houses were built for airmen and their families.

Fonmon
The Castle 1899
43464
Fonmon Castle was built
by the Anglo-Norman
St John family. Through
marriage they became
related to the royal
house of Tudor. In 1622,
Oliver St John of Bletsoe
(Fonmon was his
secondary residence)
commissioned maps of
his lands in Wales, and
these form a valuable
record of land in the
Vale of Glamorgan.
Colonel Philip Jones
bought the estate in the
1650s. Oliver Jones
(1813-1878) is reputed
to have brought the first
Pekinese dogs into this
country.

Aberthaw, Burton Bridge 1899 43469
The Methodists held their services in Burton House in this village.

Aberthaw, The Village 1899 43470
Large quantities of lead from mines at Llangam and Llantrisant were exported from the port of Aberthaw during the 17th and 18th centuries. Coal is still taken to Aberthaw for the Aberthaw Power Station. The lias limestone of the cliffs at Aberthaw makes excellent cement, and the Aberthaw and Bristol Channel Cement Co established their cement works here in 1914.

Fonmon
The Village 1937 87965

Robert Jones of Fonmon expected his farm tenants to carry 2 sacks of coal annually for him from the pithead to his castle, and instructed his agent to let him know which tenant refused to oblige. He claimed exclusive rights over shipping corn from Aberthaw to Bristol, and put pressure on his tenants to deal only with the merchants of whom he approved. It was usual for landowners to evict any tenants who failed to pay their rent. However, Robert Jones wrote to John Franklen in 1789: 'I thought as he and his wife are very industrious that it was better to trust them with some stock than to keep the land in Hand as there is now a year's Hay on it unsold'. The Fonmon Castle estate is presently owned by Sir Hugo Boothby, who was made an Honorary Freeman of the Borough of the Vale of Glamorgan in 1984.

▼ **Rhoose, The Village Pump 1937** 87963
In 1954 Cardiff Airport was moved from Pengam Moors in the city to the former RAF station at Rhoose. The Fontygary Holiday and Leisure park at Rhoose offers luxury holiday homes for sale or hire, with bars, a health club and an indoor swimming pool.

▼ **Barry, Windsor Road 1899** 43437
The Barry Hotel occupied a corner site in Windsor Road. In 1910 there were 9 schools, free reading rooms, a library and the Theatre Royal (later used as a cinema) in Barry. The Glamorgan Residential Women's Teacher Training College opened in 1914. By 1920 the town's population had increased to nearly 40,000.

▲ **Barry 1900** 45548
This photograph conveys the pleasure to be gained from a day at the seaside with rocks to sit on, a driftwood fire to heat water for a picnic, and parasols to prevent damaging that fashionably pale complexion.

◄ **Barry**
Broad Street 1899 43433
In 1841 there were 12
households in Barry, and in
1861 the population was
less than 100. But the
development of the dock
triggered phenomenal
growth, with the building of
shops, churches, and
houses. The Masonic Hall
was situated here in Broad
Street, and so was the
London Provincial Bank
(left).

Barry
The Dock 1899 43451
The Barry Dock and
Railways Company, which
became the largest
integrated dock and
railway company in Great
Britain, was formed in
1884. Colliery owners,
dissatisfied with increased
costs at Cardiff, decided
to open a dock at Barry
and built it between the
mainland and Barry
Island. It was opened in
1889 and became the
greatest coal shipping
port in South Wales,
handling 11 million tons in
1913. The prime mover
involved in building the
docks was David Davies
of the Ocean Coal
Company Ltd - his statue
stands in front of the
dock offices. He was
known as 'Davies the
Ocean' and also as 'Top
Sawyer', a nickname
earned from his youthful
employment at a saw-pit
where he worked at the
top of the sawpit, not at
the bottom where the
sawdust fell.

Barry
Redbrink Crescent 1925 77484

In 1896 the railway was extended to Barry Island, which thus ceased to be an island, now that there was a road and railway built on the causeway. Collin's fairground with the famous 'figure eight' railway opened in 1924. Soon the economic depression caused unemployment at the docks, and the Barry Development Committee was set up in 1925, hoping to develop Barry as a seaside resort. The Great Western Railway advertised excursions from as far afield as London and the Midlands. After the war, some residents resented the crowds - nearly 100,000 people - that arrived in charabancs at the weekends. A Mr Austin Beynon complained in a letter to the press that he had bought a large house on the island in 1899 when the location was the 'fairest place on earth', but now with vast crowds, silver bands, roundabouts and so on, who would want to buy it? An answer was printed from 'Anonymous Bandsman', reminding him that many ex-servicemen were forced to live in filthy conditions packed in houses like sardines in a box, and suggesting that he should have bought the whole island and fenced himself in.

Barry, Whitmore Bay 1910 62559
On weekdays the main railway line from the Rhondda valley to Barry carried coal to the docks, but it was used on Sundays and bank holidays by excursion trains to the seaside.

St Fagans, The Stepping Stones 1906 56486
The Museum of Welsh Life opened in 1948 with Iorwerth Peate as curator. The castle, on a crag above the river Ely, was founded by the Norman Le Sor family and was the residence of the Earl of Plymouth. He presented it with its gardens and grounds to the folk museum in 1947. Among the buildings on view are the 16th-century dovecot, and examples of dwellings from different counties and different centuries, all painstakingly rebuilt and furnished. School parties come here to dress in Victorian clothes and take lessons in the Victorian schoolroom, and adults can watch cookery demonstrations in the vast castle kitchen. Workers' cottages from Merthyr are furnished to show what was fashionable at various periods, and visitors can go back in time when they enter the village shop.

Dinas Powys
Highwalls Avenue c1955
D31054
In medieval times, Dinas Powys was the administrative centre of the hundred of Dinas Powys, which was composed of 26 parishes. General Lee, lord of the manor, erected a parish room for villagers, but he closed it when he heard that cards were being played for money there. The ruins of the Norman castle were acquired by the local Civic Trust in 1982.

Lavernock
The Caravan Site c1955 L279017
A tablet on the church wall at Lavernock states: 'Near this spot the first radio message was exchanged across the water by Guglielmo Marconi and George Kemp between Lavernock and Flat Holm, 11th May, and Lavernock and Brean Down, 18th May 1897'. Nearby is Cosmeton Country Park, with watersports on lakes created in disused quarries. Gypsum was mined along the coast between Penarth and Lavernock.

▼ Sully
Station Road c1955
S437008
The coming of the railway made Sully beaches accessible to workers from Cardiff as well as from the mining towns. Visitors to Sully Hospital, opened in 1936 to treat tuberculosis sufferers, and now closed, used it too.

◄ Sully
Swan Bridge Beach c1955 S437005
The lovely beach at Swanbridge was reputed to be more popular than Penarth at the beginning of the 20th century. With romantic tree-sheltered pathways, rock pools and shallows for paddling, it had something for all the family.

Penarth
The Beach 1896 38462
Harriet Windsor-Clive, the Countess of Plymouth, took an interest in the layout of Penarth. (The Windsor family owned most of the land in the district). In 1868 the Penarth hotel, designed by C E Bernard, was built by the Taff Vale Railway Company. It later became the Headlands School. Wealthy coal magnates and shipping owners built their villas at Penarth. Penarth Dock had a special 4-tip berth which enabled dockers to load a ship with 4,000 tons of coal in a few hours. The dock closed in 1936, though it was used for a period during the war. The 'Waverley' (a paddle steamer) and the 'Balmoral' (a cruise ship) sail from Penarth pier during the summer months.

Vaynor
General View c1965
V12093
In the churchyard of
Vaynor parish church,
in the hamlet of
Pontsarn, lies the tomb
of Richard Crawshay,
former iron master of
Cyfarthfa: a ten-ton slab
of stone over his grave
bears the words 'God
forgive me'. The farms
of this upland area
produced food for the
workers of Merthyr,
many of whom lived in
houses built on
Cefncoed, which
became a dormitory for
Merthyr.

Llandough, The Merry Harrier c1955 L280007
When Theodore Mansel Talbot started the Glamorganshire Hunt, he established hunt kennels and stables at Llandough, so the public house is aptly named. In 1803 minerals were mined on the Earl of Bute's estate at Llandough: there were alabaster, fuller's earth and black marble workings.

Marcross, The Bungalow 1936 87825
Tea-rooms were opened in seaside villages during the 1930s. Many tourists came here to visit the caves in the limestone cliffs of Tresilian Bay near Marcross. According to legend, you could predict how soon you would marry by seeing how far you could throw a pebble into a certain cave. The parents of General Picton, who was killed at Waterloo, were married in one of the caves.

Merthyr Tydfil
The Public Library c1960 M118035

Merthyr Tydfil was described as a 'miserable straggling village' in the 1760s. By 1860 it was
the principal town of Wales, and the iron-making capital of the world. Cholera outbreaks in
Merthyr and other towns led to the construction of reservoirs at Pentwyn. In June 1831
there occurred a mass rising at Merthyr, precipitated by the truck system and The Court of
Requests and cuts in wages. Thousands of iron-workers under a red flag destroyed a
debtor's court and called a general strike at the ironworks, demanding Reform. They were
eventually defeated by troops after twice forcing the soldiers to retreat, and 28 scapegoats
were tried for rioting. One man, a 23-year-old miner, was hanged. He was Dic Penderyn
(Richard Lewis), and his last word on the gallows was 'Injustice'. In 1900 Keir Hardy was
elected as MP for Merthyr, becoming the first Labour MP in Britain.

Merthyr Tydfil
Cyfarthfa Castle c1955 M118041
Cyfarthfa Castle was built in 1825 by William Crawshay. He was the grandson
of Richard Crawshay, owner of Cyfarthfa ironworks, and one of the
industrialists who caused the construction of the canal linking Merthyr with
Cardiff. The county borough of Merthyr Tydfil bought the castle in 1909, and
set up a grammar school in part of it. It now houses a museum and art gallery,
and offers an education service and conference/corporate hospitality.

St Nicholas, Dyffryn House and Gardens c1965 S436003
Dyffryn House was built in 1893 by coal magnate John Cory on the site of an older house. When he died in 1910, his son Reginald continued to develop the gardens, engaging an architect to redesign them and introducing rare plants. Among the garden 'rooms' there is a Pompeian garden within arcades of pillars.

Tongwynlais, Castell Coch c1960 T188003
Castell Coch was a fortress built by Gilbert de Clare around 1260 on the site of an earlier Welsh stronghold owned by Ifor ap Meurig, the Welsh Lord of Senghennydd, affectionately known as Ifor Bach (there is a Cardiff club named after him). In 1871 Lord Bute, with his architect Burgess, rebuilt the castle on the ruins of de Clare's castle. It has cylindrical towers with conical roofs, and has been described as a 'wild Wagnerian fantasy'. Lady Bute's bedroom, on two floors, and the octagonal drawing room are richly decorated with carvings and paintings.

Llantrisant
The Church c1965 L286038
The church is dedicated to three saints, Illtyd, Gwyno and Dyfed,
and was built in 1096. When the church was being renovated in
1893, a foundry was found under the tower, in which were the
moulds that had been used for casting the bells in 1718. In 1884
Dr William Price of Llantrisant was arrested and tried for attempting
to burn his son's body on Llantrisant common. His acquittal led to
the legalisation of cremation. The Royal Mint was opened here in
1968; the first coin was struck by the queen.

Caerphilly
The Castle c1874 7032
Gilbert de Clare built it; Llywelyn ap Gruffudd destroyed it; Gilbert
started to rebuild it, but it took 100 years for the work to be
completed. It covers 30 acres, and it is said that one tower leans over
further than the tower of Pisa. The Bute family owned the castle in
1776, and restored parts of it. In 1950 it was transferred to the
Department of the Environment, who completed the restoration. It has
a banqueting hall and full-sized working replicas of medieval siege
engines, and is said to be haunted by the ghost of the Green Lady.

Cardiff
The Docks 1893 32696
The opening of the
Glamorgan Canal from
Merthyr Tydfil in 1794,
and of the West Bute
Dock in 1839, and the
coming of the railway,
helped to change
Cardiff from a seaside
village to the largest
town in Wales. By 1901
its population had risen
to 164,330 and it was
the most important coal
exporting port in
Britain.

Cardiff
Queen Street 1897
38997
Before the town council renamed it Queen Street, this road was called Crockherbtown, allegedly because the monks of Greyfriars used to grow pots of herbs here. The last Cardiff tram ran in 1950. Mr Morgan promised painless dentistry here in 1897 - note his sign on the left.

▼ **Cardiff, High Street 1893** 32675
St Mary's Street is featured in the foreground of this photograph, with High Street in the background and the indoor market between them. On the left is the Great Western Hotel designed by W D Bessley in 1876, and further North is the Royal Hotel built in 1866 to C E Bernard's design. The National Provincial Bank occupied 5 High Street in 1835, having opened in 1792 on the opposite side of the street, on the site of the present Lloyd's Bank. Delightful arcades with elegant upper storeys and glass roofs link these two streets with other Cardiff streets. James Howells's department store, now a House of Fraser Store is at 14 St Mary's Street and Morgan's Arcade leads to David Morgan's department store in the Hayes.

▼ **Cardiff, The Ruins, Cathays Park c1955** C23077
This photograph shows the remains of the Tudor mansion that the Herbert family built in the ruins of the old Friary where the monks had once grown herbs in Crockherbtown. The Herberts (the Earls of Pembroke) acquired the site after the dissolution of the monasteries in the reign of Henry VIII.

▲ **Cardiff
The Castle, the South Front c1900** 32670a
One of the best preserved examples of a Norman motte and keep can be seen inside the grounds of Cardiff Castle. The 3rd Marquess of Bute employed the architect William Burgess to redesign Cardiff Castle in 1868. Highly-coloured and gilded walls and ceilings and tiled floors and exotic wood help to make it a romantic Victorian fantasy.

◄ **Llandaff
The Cathedral 1893**

32698

Llandaff Cathedral, founded by St Teilo in the 6th century, lies in a hollow, sited so as to be shielded from the Vikings. Inside, a parabolic arch made of dyed concrete holds aloft the aluminium statue of Christ in Majesty by Epstein, erected in 1957.

Bargoed, High Street 1951 B300022
Bargoed was named after Bargoed Junction on the Rhymney Valley line. The viaduct leading to Bargoed Junction was built in 1858. According to the Western Mail of 2 February 2002, more than £1000,000 in Objective One funding is going towards an internet cafe in Bargoed. The slagheaps are now forested.

Senghennydd, Commercial Street c1965 S440009
439 men and boys were killed in an explosion at the Universal Colliery, Senghennydd on 14 October 1913, and 45 of those had lived in Commercial Street. Nearly every family in the village suffered losses. An inquiry into the disaster concluded that safety laws had been broken. At an earlier disaster at the same pit in 1901, 81 miners lost their lives.

Rumney
The Village c1955 R297002
Rumney is proud of its village atmosphere: in 1950 Leslie Batten in
his advertisements described himself as 'The Country Butcher'. Eddie
Price built up a prosperous haulage business as road traffic took over
from the railway, having started off with one vehicle in 1932.

Rumney
A Housing Estate c1965 R297001
In the rag magazine of Cardiff University in 1958,
J North & Son, builder and contractor of Rumney,
promised: 'Whatever you need - from a mouse-trap to a
skyscraper, give the building job to them and - relax'.

Index

Frith Book Co Titles

www.francisfrith.co.uk

The Frith Book Company publishes over 100 new titles each year. A selection of those currently available is listed below. For latest catalogue please contact Frith Book Co.

Town Books 96 pages, approximately 100 photos. **County and Themed Books** 128 pages, approximately 150 photos (unless specified). All titles hardback with laminated case and jacket, except those indicated pb (paperback)

Amersham, Chesham & Rickmansworth (pb)	1-85937-340-2	£9.99	Derbyshire Living Memories	1-85937-330-5	£14.99
Andover (pb)	1-85937-292-9	£9.99	Devon Churches (pb)	1-85937-250-3	£9.99
Aylesbury (pb)	1-85937-227-9	£9.99	Dorchester (pb)	1-85937-307-0	£9.99
Barnstaple (pb)	1-85937-300-3	£9.99	Dorset (pb)	1-85937-269-4	£9.99
Basildon Living Memories (pb)	1-85937-515-4	£9.99	Down the Severn (pb)	1-85937-560-x	£9.99
Bath (pb)	1-85937-419-0	£9.99	Down The Thames (pb)	1-85937-278-3	£9.99
Bedford (pb)	1-85937-205-8	£9.99	Down the Trent	1-85937-311-9	£14.99
Bedfordshire Living Memories	1-85937-513-8	£14.99	East Anglia (pb)	1-85937-265-1	£9.99
Belfast (pb)	1-85937-303-8	£9.99	East Grinstead (pb)	1-85937-138-8	£9.99
Berkshire (pb)	1-85937-191-4	£9.99	East Sussex (pb)	1-85937-606-1	£9.99
Berkshire Churches	1-85937-170-1	£17.99	Eastbourne (pb)	1-85937-399-2	£9.99
Berkshire Living Memories	1-85937-332-1	£14.99	Edinburgh (pb)	1-85937-193-0	£8.99
Blackpool (pb)	1-85937-393-3	£9.99	Essex - Second Selection	1-85937-456-5	£14.99
Bognor Regis (pb)	1-85937-431-x	£9.99	Essex (pb)	1-85937-270-8	£9.99
Bournemouth (pb)	1-85937-545-6	£9.99	Essex Coast	1-85937-342-9	£14.99
Bradford (pb)	1-85937-204-x	£9.99	Essex Living Memories	1-85937-490-5	£14.99
Bridgend (pb)	1-85937-386-0	£7.99	Exeter	1-85937-539-1	£9.99
Bridgwater (pb)	1-85937-305-4	£9.99	Exmoor (pb)	1-85937-608-8	£9.99
Bridport (pb)	1-85937-327-5	£9.99	Falmouth (pb)	1-85937-594-4	£9.99
Brighton (pb)	1-85937-192-2	£8.99	Folkestone (pb)	1-85937-124-8	£9.99
Bristol (pb)	1-85937-264-3	£9.99	Frome (pb)	1-85937-317-8	£9.99
British Life A Century Ago (pb)	1-85937-213-9	£9.99	Glamorgan	1-85937-488-3	£14.99
Buckinghamshire (pb)	1-85937-200-7	£9.99	Glasgow (pb)	1-85937-190-6	£9.99
Camberley (pb)	1-85937-222-8	£9.99	Glastonbury (pb)	1-85937-338-0	£7.99
Cambridge (pb)	1-85937-422-0	£9.99	Gloucester (pb)	1-85937-232-5	£9.99
Cambridgeshire (pb)	1-85937-420-4	£9.99	Gloucestershire (pb)	1-85937-561-8	£9.99
Cambridgeshire Villages	1-85937-523-5	£14.99	Greater Manchester (pb)	1-85937-266-x	£9.99
Canals And Waterways (pb)	1-85937-291-0	£9.99	Guildford (pb)	1-85937-410-7	£9.99
Canterbury Cathedral (pb)	1-85937-179-5	£9.99	Hampshire (pb)	1-85937-279-1	£9.99
Carmarthenshire (pb)	1-85937-604-5	£9.99	Harrogate (pb)	1-85937-423-9	£9.99
Chelmsford (pb)	1-85937-310-0	£9.99	Hastings and Bexhill (pb)	1-85937-131-0	£9.99
Cheltenham (pb)	1-85937-095-0	£9.99	Heart of Lancashire (pb)	1-85937-197-3	£9.99
Cheshire (pb)	1-85937-271-6	£9.99	Helston (pb)	1-85937-214-7	£9.99
Chester (pb)	1-85937-382-8	£9.99	Hereford (pb)	1-85937-175-2	£9.99
Chesterfield (pb)	1-85937-378-x	£9.99	Herefordshire (pb)	1-85937-567-7	£9.99
Chichester (pb)	1-85937-228-7	£9.99	Herefordshire Living Memories	1-85937-514-6	£14.99
Churches of East Cornwall (pb)	1-85937-249-x	£9.99	Hertfordshire (pb)	1-85937-247-3	£9.99
Churches of Hampshire (pb)	1-85937-207-4	£9.99	Horsham (pb)	1-85937-432-8	£9.99
Cinque Ports & Two Ancient Towns	1-85937-492-1	£14.99	Humberside (pb)	1-85937-605-3	£9.99
Colchester (pb)	1-85937-188-4	£8.99	Hythe, Romney Marsh, Ashford (pb)	1-85937-256-2	£9.99
Cornwall Living Memories	1-85937-248-1	£14.99	Ipswich (pb)	1-85937-424-7	£9.99
Cotswolds (pb)	1-85937-230-9	£9.99	Isle of Man (pb)	1-85937-268-6	£9.99
Cotswolds Living Memories	1-85937-255-4	£14.99	Isle of Wight (pb)	1-85937-429-8	£9.99
County Durham (pb)	1-85937-398-4	£9.99	Isle of Wight Living Memories	1-85937-304-6	£14.99
Croydon Living Memories (pb)	1-85937-162-0	£9.99	Kent (pb)	1-85937-189-2	£9.99
Derby (pb)	1-85937-367-4	£9.99	Kent Living Memories(pb)	1-85937-401-8	£9.99
Derbyshire (pb)	1-85937-196-5	£9.99	Kings Lynn (pb)	1-85937-334-8	£9.99

Available from your local bookshop or from the publisher

Frith Book Co Titles (continued)

Title	ISBN	Price	Title	ISBN	Price
Leicester (pb)	1-85937-381-x	£9.99	Sherborne (pb)	1-85937-301-1	£9.99
Leicestershire & Rutland Living Memories	1-85937-500-6	£12.99	Shrewsbury (pb)	1-85937-325-9	£9.99
Leicestershire (pb)	1-85937-185-x	£9.99	Shropshire (pb)	1-85937-326-7	£9.99
Lighthouses	1-85937-257-0	£9.99	Shropshire Living Memories	1-85937-643-6	£14.99
Lincoln (pb)	1-85937-380-1	£9.99	South Devon Living Memories (pb)	1-85937-609-6	£9.99
Lincolnshire (pb)	1-85937-433-6	£9.99	South East London (pb)	1-85937-263-5	£9.99
Liverpool and Merseyside (pb)	1-85937-234-1	£9.99	South Somerset	1-85937-318-6	£14.99
London (pb)	1-85937-183-3	£9.99	South Wales	1-85937-519-7	£14.99
London Living Memories	1-85937-454-9	£14.99	Southampton (pb)	1-85937-427-1	£9.99
Ludlow (pb)	1-85937-176-0	£9.99	Southport (pb)	1-85937-425-5	£9.99
Luton (pb)	1-85937-235-x	£9.99	St Albans (pb)	1-85937-341-0	£9.99
Maidenhead (pb)	1-85937-339-9	£9.99	St Ives (pb)	1-85937-415-8	£9.99
Maidstone (pb)	1-85937-391-7	£9.99	Stafford Living Memories (pb)	1-85937-503-0	£9.99
Marlborough (pb)	1-85937-336-4	£9.99	Staffordshire (pb)	1-85937-308-9	£9.99
Middlesex	1-85937-158-2	£14.99	Stourbridge (pb)	1-85937-530-8	£9.99
Monmouthshire	1-85937-532-4	£14.99	Stratford upon Avon (pb)	1-85937-388-7	£9.99
New Forest (pb)	1-85937-390-9	£9.99	Suffolk (pb)	1-85937-221-x	£9.99
Newark (pb)	1-85937-366-6	£9.99	Suffolk Coast (pb)	1-85937-610-x	£9.99
Newquay (pb)	1-85937-421-2	£9.99	Surrey (pb)	1-85937-240-6	£9.99
Norfolk (pb)	1-85937-195-7	£9.99	Surrey Living Memories	1-85937-328-3	£14.99
Norfolk Broads	1-85937-486-7	£14.99	Sussex (pb)	1-85937-184-1	£9.99
Norfolk Living Memories (pb)	1-85937-402-6	£9.99	Sutton (pb)	1-85937-337-2	£9.99
North Buckinghamshire	1-85937-626-6	£14.99	Swansea (pb)	1-85937-167-1	£9.99
North Devon Living Memories	1-85937-261-9	£14.99	Taunton (pb)	1-85937-314-3	£9.99
North Hertfordshire	1-85937-547-2	£14.99	Tees Valley & Cleveland (pb)	1-85937-623-1	£9.99
North London (pb)	1-85937-403-4	£9.99	Teignmouth (pb)	1-85937-370-4	£7.99
North Somerset	1-85937-302-x	£14.99	Thanet (pb)	1-85937-116-7	£9.99
North Wales (pb)	1-85937-298-8	£9.99	Tiverton (pb)	1-85937-178-7	£9.99
North Yorkshire (pb)	1-85937-236-8	£9.99	Torbay (pb)	1-85937-597-9	£9.99
Northamptonshire Living Memories	1-85937-529-4	£14.99	Truro (pb)	1-85937-598-7	£9.99
Northamptonshire	1-85937-150-7	£14.99	Victorian & Edwardian Dorset	1-85937-254-6	£14.99
Northumberland	1-85937-522-7	£14.99	Victorian & Edwardian Kent (pb)	1-85937-624-X	£9.99
Norwich (pb)	1-85937-194-9	£8.99	Victorian & Edwardian Maritime Album (pb)	1-85937-622-3	£9.99
Nottingham (pb)	1-85937-324-0	£9.99	Victorian and Edwardian Sussex (pb)	1-85937-625-8	£9.99
Nottinghamshire (pb)	1-85937-187-6	£9.99	Villages of Devon (pb)	1-85937-293-7	£9.99
Oxford (pb)	1-85937-411-5	£9.99	Villages of Kent (pb)	1-85937-294-5	£9.99
Oxfordshire (pb)	1-85937-430-1	£9.99	Warrington (pb)	1-85937-507-3	£9.99
Oxfordshire Living Memories	1-85937-525-1	£14.99	Warwick (pb)	1-85937-518-9	£9.99
Paignton (pb)	1-85937-374-7	£7.99	Welsh Castles (pb)	1-85937-322-4	£9.99
Peak District (pb)	1-85937-280-5	£9.99	West Yorkshire (pb)	1-85937-201-5	£9.99
Penzance (pb)	1-85937-595-2	£9.99	Weymouth (pb)	1-85937-209-0	£9.99
Peterborough (pb)	1-85937-219-8	£9.99	Wiltshire (pb)	1-85937-277-5	£9.99
Picturesque Harbours	1-85937-208-2	£14.99	Wiltshire Churches (pb)	1-85937-171-x	£9.99
Piers	1-85937-237-6	£17.99	Wiltshire Living Memories (pb)	1-85937-396-8	£9.99
Plymouth (pb)	1-85937-389-5	£9.99	Winchester (pb)	1-85937-428-x	£9.99
Poole & Sandbanks (pb)	1-85937-251-1	£9.99	Windsor (pb)	1-85937-333-x	£9.99
Redhill to Reigate (pb)	1-85937-596-0	£9.99	Wokingham & Bracknell (pb)	1-85937-329-1	£9.99
Ringwood (pb)	1-85937-384-4	£7.99	Woodbridge (pb)	1-85937-498-0	£9.99
Romford (pb)	1-85937-319-4	£9.99	Worcester (pb)	1-85937-165-5	£9.99
Royal Tunbridge Wells (pb)	1-85937-504-9	£9.99	York (pb)	1-85937-199-x	£9.99
Salisbury (pb)	1-85937-239-2	£9.99	Yorkshire (pb)	1-85937-186-8	£9.99
Scarborough (pb)	1-85937-379-8	£9.99	Yorkshire Coastal Memories	1-85937-506-5	£14.99
Sevenoaks and Tonbridge (pb)	1-85937-392-5	£9.99	Yorkshire Dales	1-85937-502-2	£14.99

See Frith books on the internet at www.francisfrith.co.uk

FRITH PRODUCTS & SERVICES

Francis Frith would doubtless be pleased to know that the pioneering publishing venture he started in 1860 still continues today. Over a hundred and forty years later, The Francis Frith Collection continues in the same innovative tradition and is now one of the foremost publishers of vintage photographs in the world. Some of the current activities include:

Interior Decoration

Today Frith's photographs can be seen framed and as giant wall murals in thousands of pubs, restaurants, hotels, banks, retail stores and other public buildings throughout the country. In every case they enhance the unique local atmosphere of the places they depict and provide reminders of gentler days in an increasingly busy and frenetic world.

Product Promotions

Frith products are used by many major companies to promote the sales of their own products or to reinforce their own history and heritage. Frith promotions have been used by Hovis bread, Courage beers, Scots Porage Oats, Colman's mustard, Cadbury's foods, Mellow Birds coffee, Dunhill pipe tobacco, Guinness, and Bulmer's Cider.

Genealogy and Family History

As the interest in family history and roots grows world-wide, more and more people are turning to Frith's photographs of Great Britain for images of the towns, villages and streets where their ancestors lived; and, of course, photographs of the churches and chapels where their ancestors were christened, married and buried are an essential part of every genealogy tree and family album.

Frith Products

All Frith photographs are available Framed or just as Mounted Prints and Posters (size 23 x 16 inches). These may be ordered from the address below. From time to time other products - Address Books, Maps, etc - are available.

The Internet

Already fifty thousand Frith photographs can be viewed and purchased on the internet through the Frith websites and a myriad of partner sites.

For more detailed information on Frith companies and products, look at these sites:

www.francisfrith.co.uk
www.francisfrith.com
(for North American visitors)

See the complete list of Frith Books at:

www.francisfrith.co.uk

This web site is regularly updated with the latest list of publications from the Frith Book Company. If you wish to buy books relating to another part of the country that your local bookshop does not stock, you may purchase on-line.

For further information, trade, or author enquiries please contact us at the address below:
The Francis Frith Collection, Frith's Barn, Teffont, Salisbury, Wiltshire, England SP3 5QP.
Tel: +44 (0)1722 716 376 Fax: +44 (0)1722 716 881 Email: sales@francisfrith.co.uk

See Frith books on the internet at www.francisfrith.co.uk

FREE PRINT OF YOUR CHOICE

Mounted Print
Overall size 14 x 11 inches (355 x 280mm)

Choose any Frith photograph in this book.
Simply complete the Voucher opposite and return it with your remittance for £2.25 (to cover postage and handling) and we will print the photograph of your choice in SEPIA (size 11 x 8 inches) and supply it in a cream mount with a burgundy rule line (overall size 14 x 11 inches).
Please note: photographs with a reference number starting with a "Z" are not Frith photographs and cannot be supplied under this offer.
Offer valid for delivery to one UK address only.

**PLUS: Order additional Mounted Prints
at HALF PRICE - £7.49 each** (normally £14.99)
If you would like to order more Frith prints from this book, possibly as gifts for friends and family, you can buy them at half price (with no additional postage and handling costs).

PLUS: Have your Mounted Prints framed
For an extra £14.95 per print you can have your mounted print(s) framed in an elegant polished wood and gilt moulding, overall size 16 x 13 inches (no additional postage and handling required).

IMPORTANT!

These special prices are only available if you use this form to order . You must use the ORIGINAL VOUCHER on this page (no copies permitted). We can only despatch to one UK address. This offer cannot be combined with any other offer.

Send completed Voucher form to:
The Francis Frith Collection, Frith's Barn, Teffont, Salisbury, Wiltshire SP3 5QP

CHOOSE A PHOTOGRAPH FROM THIS BOOK

Voucher for **FREE** *and Reduced Price Frith Prints*

Please do not photocopy this voucher. Only the original is valid, so please fill it in, cut it out and return it to us with your order.

Picture ref no	Page no	Qty	Mounted @ £7.49	Framed + £14.95	Total Cost £
		1	Free of charge*	£	£
			£7.49	£	£
			£7.49	£	£
			£7.49	£	£
			£7.49	£	£
			£7.49	£	£

*Please allow 28 days for delivery.
Offer available to one UK address only*

* Post & handling	£2.25	
Total Order Cost	£	

Title of this book . . . .
I enclose a cheque/postal order for £ . . . .
made payable to 'The Francis Frith Collection'

OR please debit my Mastercard / Visa / Maestro / Amex card, details below

Card Number

Issue No (Maestro only)   Valid from (Maestro)

Expires   Signature

Name Mr/Mrs/Ms . . . .
Address . . . .
. . . .
. . . .
. . . . Postcode . . . .
Daytime Tel No . . . .
Email . . . .

Valid to 31/12/07

Free Print – see overleaf

Would you like to find out more about Francis Frith?

We have recently recruited some entertaining speakers who are happy to visit local groups, clubs and societies to give an illustrated talk documenting Frith's travels and photographs. If you are a member of such a group and are interested in hosting a presentation, we would love to hear from you.

Our speakers bring with them a small selection of our local town and county books, together with sample prints. They are happy to take orders. A small proportion of the order value is donated to the group who have hosted the presentation. The talks are therefore an excellent way of fundraising for small groups and societies.

Can you help us with information about any of the Frith photographs in this book?

We are gradually compiling an historical record for each of the photographs in the Frith archive. It is always fascinating to find out the names of the people shown in the pictures, as well as insights into the shops, buildings and other features depicted.

If you recognize anyone in the photographs in this book, or if you have information not already included in the author's caption, do let us know. We would love to hear from you, and will try to publish it in future books or articles.

Our production team

Frith books are produced by a small dedicated team at offices in the converted Grade II listed 18th-century barn at Teffont near Salisbury, illustrated above. Most have worked with the Frith Collection for many years. All have in common one quality: they have a passion for the Frith Collection. The team is constantly expanding, but currently includes:

Paul Baron, Phillip Brennan, Jason Buck, John Buck, Ruth Butler, Heather Crisp, David Davies, Louis du Mont, Isobel Hall, Gareth Harris, Lucy Hart, Julian Hight, Peter Horne, James Kinnear, Karen Kinnear, Tina Leary, Stuart Login, David Marsh, Lesley-Ann Millard, Sue Molloy, Glenda Morgan, Wayne Morgan, Sarah Roberts, Kate Rotondetto, Dean Scource, Eliza Sackett, Terence Sackett, Sandra Sampson, Adrian Sanders, Sandra Sanger, Jan Scrivens, Julia Skinner, David Smith, Miles Smith, Lewis Taylor, Shelley Tolcher, Lorraine Tuck, Amanita Wainwright and Ricky Williams.